THE BEST OF BRITAIN HERITAGE SERIES
Lancashire's Hill Co...

The Irwell Valley above Ramsbottom

CONTENTS

- **4** INTRODUCTION TO THE AREA
- **5** THE GEOLOGY OF THE AREA
- **6** LANDFORMS TO VISIT
- **9** INVASION, SETTLEMENT & WAR
- **10** THE PENDLE WITCHES
- **11** THE INDUSTRIAL REVOLUTION
- **12** CANALS & RAILWAYS
- **13** ANNUAL EVENTS & CUSTOMS
- **14** FARMING PAST & PRESENT
- **15** LOCAL LEGENDS & DIALECT
- **16** TICS, INFORMATION & MAP
- **18** OUTDOOR ACTIVITIES
- **19** THE RICHES OF NATURE
- **21** HISTORIC BUILDINGS
- **23** MUSEUMS & GALLERIES
- **26** TOWNS & VILLAGES OF THE AREA
- **29** TWO GARDEN NURSERIES

Cover photographs: (Top) The River Hodder at Whitewell near Clitheroe; (Bottom Left) Picnickers enjoying the view from Jeffry Hill; (Bottom Right) Heather hills above the Trough of Bowland.

Discovery Publishing (UK) Limited wish to thank all those persons, organisations, official bodies and their officers, for their kind assistance in the production of this publication.

Photographs reproduced by kind permission of Discovery Photo Library Ltd. (Photographer: Philip Loudon). Photograph marked (BP) reproduced courtesy of Borough of Pendle. Photograph marked (HC) reproduced courtesy of Holden Clough Nursery.

All rights reserved. No part of this publication may be reproduced, stored in a retrieval system or transmitted in any form or by any means, without the prior written permission of the Copyright Owner.

The author and publishers of this book do not accept any responsibility for the accuracy of the general information, tours and routes suggested for travellers by road or on foot and no guarantee is given that the routes and tours suggested are still available when this book is read. Readers should take all elementary precautions such as checking road and weather conditions before embarking on recommended routes and tours. Any persons using the information in this guide do so entirely at their own discretion.

WRITTEN BY RACHEL M. HOLT AND CAROLINE HILLERY. EDITED BY CAROLINE HILLERY. SERIES EDITOR AND DESIGN MALCOLM PARKER. ARTWORK AND DESIGN ANDREW FALLON. PUBLISHED BY DISCOVERY PUBLISHING (UK) LTD., 1 MARKET PLACE, MIDDLETON-IN-TEESDALE, CO. DURHAM, DL12 0QG. TEL: (0833) 40638. PRINTED IN ENGLAND. ISBN 0-86309-102-4. COPYRIGHT DISCOVERY PUBLISHING (UK) LTD.

Introduction to the Area

'There is plenty of smoke in Lancashire. But there is also an abundance of heather. Round every Lancashire town there is a bonny expanse of hill and fell. Lancashire is a country of sweet moorlands, with the factory towns built in their basins and valleys....'
Allen Clarke (1920).

The inner area of Lancashire is countryside of unique natural beauty, wild moorlands, spectacular woodlands and picturesque villages. It is hard to accept that all this lies no more than 25 miles (40 kms) north of the busy industrial city of Manchester and almost equidistant from the cotton towns of Preston and Halifax. It is impossible not to fall under the spell of this breathtaking landscape, liberally sprinkled with an abundance of historic buildings and hemmed in by the wild **Pennine Hills** and the rustic **Fells of Bowland**.

Lancashire's Hill Country is comprised of six boroughs: **Rossendale, Ribble Valley, Blackburn, Burnley, Pendle** and **Hyndburn**, each offering its own brand of charm and historic interest and an opportunity to capture a flavour of the Industrial Revolution.

Picturesque Whitewell in the Hodder Valley

THE INDUSTRIAL REVOLUTION transformed Lancashire's Hill Country by giving it a reputation for smoky mill chimneys and declining industries. Today, this could not be further from the truth, with the famed working mill chimney now something of a collector's item. The majority are merely redundant reminders of a distant past, there for the enjoyment of those seeking a snapshot of a different period in time. It is difficult not to be affected by the addictive atmosphere of this past era which was so influential in shaping the development of industrial Britain.

Jubilee Tower above Tockholes

For those who enjoy exploring the relics of our industrial past, the area is a rich hunting ground indeed. For instance, the cotton industry which revolutionised Lancashire can be seen, well preserved in many places such as the **Queen Street Museum**, Burnley, where visitors can trace the progress of a county forging the manufacturing future of Britain.

But even if you are not an enthusiast for industrial archaeology, there is no doubt you will find Lancashire's Hill Country has much to offer. This attractive and popular area offers plenty to do for all the family, whether your pleasure is to enjoy the fresh air, look at the scenery or visit the historic houses with world famous collections such as the **Rachel Kay Shuttleworth Needlework Collection**, housed at **Gawthorpe Hall**, Padiham.

This is an area full of fascinating attractions, able to please all tastes, all ages and all moods, and you will find it hard to leave as the captivating landscape takes you under its spell. Typical of this part of the world is the friendly Lancastrian welcome, extended by people willing to share their historic heritage with you, their visitor. If you have not yet discovered Lancashire's Hill Country, then you are missing out on something which will prove very special, as you allow your imagination to transport you back in time.

The Geology of the Area

To go back to the beginnings of Lancashire's Hill Country necessitates a journey of 500 million years, to the period when **volcanic activity** forged the undulating land formations so characteristic of this beautiful area. Some 150 million years later, warm seas repeatedly covered and receded from the land, leaving behind the shells and skeletons of innumerable marine creatures, and the intermittent periods of lush vegetation creating deposits of **Carboniferous limestone.** The other abundant formation in the area is **millstone grit,** a form of sandstone which centuries later found its way as building stone into the architecture of the surrounding villages. **Jeffrey Hill,** close to Longridge, supplied much of the stone for these enigmatic buildings, and **Whittle-le-Woods quarry** supplied stone for the water-powered corn mills in the 1800s.

The famous Pendle Hill from Downham Churchyard

With an abundant source of lime, Clitheroe retains a previously abandoned limestone quarry, which has now returned to use for industrial purposes. Being of considerable geological importance, and to celebrate the re-opening of the quarry, a **Salt-Hill Quarry Geology Trail** has been arranged for the curious to witness what successive layers of rock can tell about past ages.

CLIMATIC FORCES over the centuries have weathered the peaks and valleys of **Bowland, Pendle** and **Rossendale,** with the valleys consisting of sand and boulder clay. This produced marshy areas in which successive sedimentary layers of clay gradually compacted to form **shale,** which has in recent times been used for brick making and brought about the arrival of a renowned red brick called the '**Accrington bloods'.** If, however, there was sufficient drainage, such rich, alluvial land offered an ideal opportunity for agricultural use.

The unspoilt beauty of the Trough of Bowland

A major change in appearance occurred in the course of the **Ice Age,** with the movement of glaciers widening the valleys, depositing sand and boulder clay as they melted and retreated. The rivers also subsequently modified the glacial landscape by erosion and deposition.

FOLLOWING THE ICE AGE warmer climatic conditions led to the **afforestation** of the highest areas by **oak** and **birch.** This was quickly followed by the first human settlers seeking the protection and the abundant food and water supply of these expansive wooded hillsides. In geological terms, therefore, it is only very recently that man has made his first appearance.

WITH THE SUDDEN ARRIVAL OF MAN it was only a short time before he began to turn the geological characteristics of the landscape to his own advantage. Certain areas favoured agriculture, with **crop-growing** being possible on rich lowland soils and somewhat higher land being suited to **pasture** for animals. In due course water from the steep valleys supplied power for the textile mills and hence laid the foundations for the industrial future.

Landforms to Visit

PENDLE HILL lies, according to Samuel Bamford in 1842,

> 'huge and bare like a leviathan reposing amid billows, while sweeping towards the left stretch other hills and moors all dotted with houses and marked by stone walls'.

East of Clitheroe, set amongst a number of small villages, all differing in style and character, Pendle Hill stands majestic and elegant. Severed from the Pennine chain and rising 589 metres (1,932 feet) above sea level. 7 miles (11 kms) in length and with a flat top, varying in width from 1 to 3 miles (1.5 to 5 kms), this prominent landmark offers viewpoints of bewildering beauty. It is from its table top summit that the views are at their most breathtaking. On clear days one can view the **Ribble Valley**, the **Yorkshire Dales** and, across the **Forest of Bowland**, even the southern reaches of the **Lake District**. This landscape certainly deserves the title of an **Area of Outstanding Natural Beauty**.

A breathtaking Bowland Fells panorama from Jeffry Hill

The historical factors and whispered tales which accompany Pendle Hill give it an air of uncertainty and fear which has attracted many a curious visitor over the years. For instance, why not visit the **Bronze Age burial mound** on Pendle Hill which is believed to be 7,000 years old, or the remote buildings at **Wymondhouses**, near Pendleton, where one of the founding fathers of the Congregationalists, **Thomas Jollie**, three centuries ago looked for sanctuary on the Pendle Hill slopes? He was one of the thousands evicted from their churches in 1662 and was forbidden to linger within a 5 mile (8 km) radius.

You can discover where the **Christian missionaries** penetrated Pendle Forest to preach to pagans, where the **Wars of the Roses** and the **Civil War** left their marks, or why the Hill was used as a link in a chain of beacons - fires used to warn the **Yeoman of Ribblesdale** of approaching danger or occasionally just as a celebration.

Pendle Hill is better known for its **witches**, a tale which is over three hundred and seventy years old but still captivates many a visitor. Few traces of their existence can now be seen but their names will long be remembered.

Forty years after these events, **George Fox** saw a vision of the work that God intended for him from Pendle Hill's summit and this led him to found the **Society of Friends**, later known as the **Quaker Movement**. Even to this day walkers climb Pendle Hill in the spirit of Fox, following the route he climbed in the spring of 1652.

Just as unusual as the tale of the Pendle witches is that of the **Whitworth Doctors**. They derive from the **Taylor family** who were notorious for miles around for miraculously curing diseases of both the rich and the poor. The Taylors were originally known for the treatment of horses, and one of their most recounted events was when treatment of the **Bishop of Durham** was abandoned in preference for attention to a four-legged friend!

Pendle Hill has so much to offer with its haunting tales, historic monuments and panoramic views. For the more energetic visitor there are also endless walks, discovering the abundance of wildlife, and such sporting activities as hang-gliding or dry skiing, a chance to blow the cobwebs away for ever. What a variety of attractions!

THE RIVER RIBBLE is described thus by Stukeley of Ribchester in 1725:

> 'very broad at this place, rapid and sonorous, running over its pebbles and, what is more to be lamented, over innumerable Roman antiquities; for in this long tract of time it had eaten away a third part of the city'.

True enough, it was around 1840 when workmen were excavating earth from the banks of the Ribble that they found a large quantity of **silver**, later declared a Treasure Trove. To this day it remains a puzzle as to how it got there. Maybe retreating Vikings threw the chest overboard into the river?

It seems that the River Ribble was laden with many curious and interesting finds. For instance, **fossils** of mammals of late Pleistocene times, two or three million years ago, were found at the mouths of the Ribble and the Mersey, while late in the C19th an assortment of **deers' antlers** were retrieved during the excavation of Preston Docks.

Of a more fairy-tale nature, an evil water spirit called **Peg O'Nell** lurked far beneath the slimy green weeds of all the Ribblesdale ponds. Many children were warned by their parents not to make the acquaintance of this infamous old witch but curiosity, as is often the case, got the better of them.

This **river of industry**, sweet and uncontaminated at its source, is born high in the moors, entering the County at **Nappa**. Travelling in a south-westerly direction, it dilates and proceeds to pass through the **Forest of Bowland** and past **Pendle Hill**. The River was used as an ecclesiastical boundary until 1541 and until 1858 it was used for probate border purposes. But with the passage of time the Ribble Valley enclosing the River Ribble now

> 'marks the boundary between a crowded coal mining and manufacturing district on the south, and a quiet thinly peopled farming country to the north, where coal is absent'. E.G.W. Hewlitt (1913).

Separating **Pendle Hill** from the **Forest of Bowland**, the **Ribble Valley** offers some of Lancashire's Hill Country's most intriguing and breathtaking countryside, with charming little villages, gardens by the famous landscape designer, **Capability Brown**, lovely churches, half-remembered tales and, of course, the traces of that ever prominent Industrial Revolution.

The effects of the **Industrial Revolution** have now subsided in this secluded area of natural beauty, but wherever you turn there are haunting reminders of its once dominant existence. There are many fast-flowing streams which once powered the water-wheels and hence facilitated the productivity of spinning. These now quiet mills still whisper their secrets of the industrial past.

Over the years, the Ribble Valley has successfully adapted itself to the needs of a C20th era, modern facilities are widespread and today there is something to occupy every interested visitor.

Holcombe Hill and pele tower near Ramsbottom

THE FOREST OF BOWLAND Covering a total area of 310 square miles (803 sq kms), the Forest of Bowland is actually a treeless moor. Enclosed by the **River Hodder** to the south and the **Rivers Wenning** and **Lune** to the north, Bowland was once endowed with a variety of wild animals and therefore was considered to be a highly prosperous hunting ground used by royalty, dating back to the time of the Normans. The origin of the **'Bowland'** name is uncertain. It is believed that the connection is in fact that of archery, meaning the 'land of the bow'. Other possibilities include a bow in the river or 'the land of cattle'.

More recently elected an **Area of Outstanding Natural Beauty**,

> 'The great 'forest' of Bowland is for the most part pleasant agriculture, strong ploughlands and rich pastures. There are wide expanses of un-enclosed moor which cannot have altered in spirit since the days when the area was the hunting ground of the de Lacy's'. Davis and Lees (1878).

Its cold isolated moors to the north are subjected to the elements of nature and are interestingly juxtaposed by the rambling hills and gentle pasture-land to the south. Picturesque in its contrasting beauty, Bowland was for many centuries part of the **Yorkshire** and **Northumbria** district, until 1974, when it became part of **Lancashire**.

THE TROUGH OF BOWLAND Rising from about 180 to 550 metres (600 to 1,800 ft) the Trough, bisected by the **River Hodder,** lies on the boundary of the Forest of Bowland. Marked by the **Trough Stone** which lies between Wyresdale and Bowland, and running from the village of **Abbeystead** to **Dunsop Bridge,** the Trough is considered to be one of the best and largest examples of unspoilt countryside to be seen. The Trough is actually described as a pathway from **Sykes** to **Marshaw.** To cross this pathway was once regarded as a dangerous and frightening adventure; in contrast today, with its renewed popularity, the Trough's solitude and unspoilt nature will hold you forever in its charms.

The beautiful Beacon Fell Country Park

BEACON FELL During medieval times, the Fell was used as one in a string of beacons lit, near the present day triangulation point on a Bronze Age burial mound, to warn of danger or celebrate major events. Good examples are the defeat of the **Spanish Armada** in 1588, or **Queen Elizabeth II's Silver Jubilee** in 1977. It is from this use, to signal across a large distance, that it was later named Beacon Fell. Covering a total of 75 hectares (185 acres), the Fell consists of over sixty percent coniferous woodland, and offers a wealth of panoramic views in all directions, for instance over **Snowdonia** and **North Wales,** the **Fylde Coast,** the **Lake District** and the **Isle of Man.** Rising 266 metres (873 ft) above sea level, Beacon Fell stands 8 miles (13 kms) north of Preston, west of the Bowland Fells.

Geologically the Fell is covered with a layer of durable **millstone grit** which protects the landscape from the elements and erosion. During prehistoric times Beacon Fell was carpeted with plants such as bilberry and heather, abundant with trees such as alder, oak and birch. The change in appearance which the Fell underwent was due to early **Vikings** and **Anglo-Saxon farmers** grazing their cattle and sheep on the fells. Gradually thick forest gave way to green pasture-land, which led a **Mr Joseph Smith** in 1868 to buy the Fell and maximise its farming capabilities. Forty years later **Fulwood Urban District Council** acquired the Fell as a place to collect water for **Barnsfold Reservoir,** and between 1938 and 1959 they set about restoring the 46 hectares (115 acres) of forest land which we know today. When the Fell was later owned by **Lancashire County Council** in 1969 the Forest was in a poor state and it took a long-term project of root development, disease prevention and a thinning process to restore the trees to their former glory. When you take a walk through the Forest look out for tree stumps which tell the tale of this work of restoration.

Designated as a **Country Park** in 1969 and now in the care of the **Countryside Commission,** Beacon Fell, boasting over 300,000 visitors a year, offers a fun day out for all with some of the most breathtaking views in the region.

LONGRIDGE FELL Rising 350 metres (1,148 ft) above sea level, Longridge Fell claims dramatic views of the **Ribble Valley, Bowland** and **Chipping,** and on clear days the **Isle of Man** and the **Welsh Mountains.** However the Fell is probably best known for its abundant supply of building stone which can be seen in the buildings of many local villages.

Beacon Fell and the Vale of Chipping from Jeffry Hill

CLIVIGER GORGE south of Burnley. This attractive location offers some fine scenery, overlooked by a much-photographed gritstone outcrop. The **Rockwater Bird Conservation Centre** is near at hand.

Invasion, Settlement & War

Combat in Lancashire's Hill Country has been a prevalent occurrence from as far back as the Iron Age. These events have been corroborated by findings of precious antiquities near **Nelson** and **Whalley**. Regrettably however, indications of the Romans' activities during their three centuries of occupation are buried below architecture of a subsequent era and consequently many aspects of their presence are ambiguous.

It was about 71 AD that **Agricola** commanded the Romans through Lancashire, passing **Ribchester** and the **Trough of Bowland.** In the surrounding area, the Romans had little effect on the hill farmers, however, apart from imposing taxes and establishing the all-important system of roads.

AFTER THE ROMAN TRIBULATIONS came the **Saxons** and **Vikings** in 570 AD. Travelling across the Pennines, the Anglo-Saxons chose to take up residence around the River Ribble, and many of their settlements are still evident today. Content with the elementary aspects of life, the Norsemen, who were **Irish Christians**, quickly became an integral part of the community. Important evidence of their existence has been discovered near **Whalley** in the shape of **Norse crosses**, predominantly embellished with snakes and chains.

THE WARS OF THE ROSES were fought over the thirty years from 1455 to 1485 between the **House of Lancaster,** represented by the red rose emblem, and the **House of York,** by the white. The torment began when **Richard, Duke of York**, declared the **Battle of St Albans**, in 1455, against **King Henry VI**. Richard consequently gained the throne for four years until his death at Wakefield in 1460, when his son **Edward IV** ruled for the subsequent ten years. Returning to power in 1470, Henry held the throne for merely a year before it was regained by Edward. Nicknamed the 'King-maker', the **Earl of Warwick** aided Henry to return to the throne only to be defeated once again by the enduring Edward. His death in 1483 by no means pacified the situation when Edward's brother, **Richard III**, provoked an additional uprising, but he was conquered and slaughtered at the **Battle of Bosworth** in 1485. Concluding the thirty year struggle, **Henry Tudor** married **Elizabeth of York,** the daughter of Edward IV, thus combining the red and white emblems into a single Tudor rose, the new crest for a new era of English Kings.

Samlesbury Hall to the west of Blackburn

THE CIVIL WAR (1642-1649) was a political and religious battle between **Charles I**, whose supporters were known as the **'Cavaliers'**, and Parliament under **Oliver Cromwell**, known as the **'Roundheads'**. Lancashire people, predominantly Catholic, were the target of much animosity, initiated by Parliament's approach to the Church of England and their expenditure between 1629 and 1640. The conflict centred around three battles, of which one ended in deadlock, and the other two were victories for Parliament. The conflicts came to an abrupt end when Charles I was executed for treason in January 1649. The Roundheads' overall superiority was partially due to Oliver Cromwell's **New Model Army,** a professional fighting body.

IN THE 1700s advocates of **James II** led the **Jacobite Rebellions** in support of their King. Taking their name from the Latin word for James, the Jacobites encouraged James, well known as the **'Old Pretender'**, to attack England via Lancashire. After only two weeks as the King of Lancashire, however, dual government armies instructed his assassination.

The next conflict to impinge on the County was the notorious **Industrial Revolution,** which shaped the modern Lancashire's Hill Country of today.

The Pendle Witches

Who were the Pendle witches? They were **'Nineteen Notorious' witches** who lived in the villages ambient to Pendle Hill during the reign of **James I**, a time when belief in witchcraft and skulduggery was common.

THE FOUNDER OF THE WITCHES was **Elizabeth Southern**, a married women now known as **Old Demdike**, who sold her soul to the devil and became 'the Devil's chief agent'. She was the ringleader of these frightful women and resided in **Malkin Tower** where she seduced **Elizabeth Device**, her daughter, and her grandchildren **Alizon, Jennet and James** Device into the ways of witchcraft.

Newchurch-in-Pendle - the heart of Pendle Witch Country

One of Demdike's mistakes, however, was to bring **Anne Whittle**, better known as **Chattox**, into the practising of witchcraft, as their relationship soon came to bitter rivalry, each wanting to outdo the other. These two opposing families terrorised the Pendle area and as a result many people claimed to have been blackmailed, too scared to refuse their demands. They dabbled in drugs, plants and herbs, sometimes using them for healing purposes, but accused of causing death to those who ate their poisoned pies and syllabubs. Whether or not such allegations were justified, it is believed that their rivalry came to a climax in March 1612 when **Bessie Whittle**, Chattox's daughter, broke into Demdike's home and took 'all or most of their linen clothes, half a peck of cut oatmeal and a quantity of meat.' Bessie blatantly wore the clothes to church on the following Sunday and **Roger Nowell**, the local magistrate, subsequently committed her to Lancaster Castle for this theft and other alleged crimes.

THE STORY CONTINUES IN 1612 when **Alizon Device** was begging in **Colne**. It was said that she asked a pedlar for some pins and, when refused, she devilishly commanded a black dog to lame him and it paralysed him down his left side. Later accused of witchcraft and brought before **Roger Nowell**, the **Justice at Read Hall**, she incriminated herself and Demdike, her notorious Grandmother, claiming that it was Demdike who had taught her to command a spirit to do her evil deeds. She also alleged that **Chattox** and her daughter **Anne** had used a clay image to bring about the death of a small child and that Chattox had murdered her own father **John Device**. This led to their questioning at **Ashlar House** in **Fence**. All four confessed and proudly described how their witchcraft worked. They were detained and sent to Lancaster for trial, which drove other witches in the area to attend a **Great Assembly and Feast** at **Malkin Tower** on Good Friday, 1612, to plot the release of the four held in Lancaster. Roger Nowell heard of this meeting and his investigation led to even more being sent for trial, including one **Alice Nutter** who was of social standing in the community so no one could understand why she was detained. It has been suggested that she was accused in revenge against her husband, **Richard Nutter**, the landowner of Chattox's family house. The two families had argued over the estate boundaries, causing Richard great financial loss.

THE TRIAL of the nineteen Pendle witches took only a few days; **ten were found guilty and executed** on the 20th of August 1612 on **Gallows Hill** outside Lancaster. Old Demdike escaped execution when she died in her cell at the age of ninety.

In 1633 a further seventeen people were accused of witchcraft and gaoled but were reprieved when the policy of executing witches was rescinded. After this no more Pendle folk were tried for witchcraft, though tales still continue to be told of the strange goings on.

The Industrial Revolution

The Hill Country was dramatically changed by the Industrial Revolution, both in terms of landscape and social life. The need for workers to run the factories acted as a magnet for the rurally based Lancastrians.

The Leeds-Liverpool Canal near Hoghton

The Lancashire people took pride in the fact that the coal and clean mountain water came from their County's abundant supplies and then as a result the goods that they produced were dispatched throughout the world - a very satisfying contribution!

WHEN DEMAND FOR COTTON made it necessary to achieve new levels of productivity, the challenge was met by four Lancashire men, all born within a fifty year span: **John Kay, Richard Arkwright, James Hargreaves** and **Samuel Crompton.** Hargreaves, the inventor of the **Spinning Jenny** in 1764, however, was the only one able to claim the good fortune of being born in **Stanhill**, near Oswaldtwistle, a charming small village in Lancashire's Hill Country. He played a large part in the birth of the Industrial Revolution and named the machine he invented after his daughter Jenny who, knocking over her mother's machine, accidentally revealed to Hargreaves a method of producing a machine with eight spindles, in one step increasing machine productivity by a factor of eight.

Hargreaves brought the machine age to life by the capability greatly to increase the output of thread. Unknowingly, he thereby began the chain of events which was to drive the growth of the Lancashire cotton industry, once one of the world's largest industries. Hargreaves had much to contend with, however, as his **Spinning Jenny** was not accepted at first because the benefits it brought also struck fear of redundancy into many people's hearts. Most militant were the Luddites, whose policy was to smash the machines which they saw as depriving people of jobs. But the tide of progress could not be held back, as ever, and the Spinning Jenny eventually had its major impact on cotton production. An original 'improved' Jenny can be seen at Helmshore Textile Museums.

TRACES OF THIS INDUSTRIAL REVOLUTION, which so shaped and altered Lancashire's Hill Country of today, are still evident in many mill towns and working museums in the area. There are many reminders of the County's wealth, such as a weather vane in the shape of a weaving shuttle above the dome on **St John's Church** in **Blackburn.** But of all the many places to visit if you wish to capture a snapshot of this fascinating era you should not miss the **Lewis Textile Museum** in Blackburn, a memorial to the cotton industry. Or perhaps you wish to witness and hear the Victorian weaving shed with its backdrop of noisy, busy machinery, the last traditional steam-powered weaving mill in the world. If so, you will enjoy a visit to the **Queen Street Mill,** Burnley.

Towels being woven in the traditional way at East Lancashire Towel Company at Barrowford in Pendle (BP)

Dethroned by the 1970s, **King Cotton** will always be remembered in this area which has so many memories. Indeed, the whole era can be recaptured if you can only let your imagination run loose. Even though new industries have since prospered, the Industrial Revolution will always rest in the minds of the intrigued, and will continue to attract many visitors searching for the industrial heritage of one of Britain's uniquely interesting areas.

Canals & Railways

Before combustion engines were invented, the newly formed industrial centres had a transport problem. They had to move their goods efficiently from the factories, sited to capitalise on raw materials and water power, to other market centres both in the UK and abroad. The canals solved this problem and soon spiralled out from Lancashire, thereby ensuring the market for Lancastrian products remained large.

'Lancashire was to Great Britain what the forum was to ancient Rome - the centre from which all roads led towards every principal province of the Empire'. Leo H Grindon (1892).

THE LEEDS/LIVERPOOL CANAL which is 127 miles (204 kms) long, the longest canal in Britain, was constructed from 1770 to 1816 at the height of the canal-building boom and was the only navigable route across the Pennines. Constructed by **Jessop, Telford** and **Whitworth,** the Canal presented new engineering hurdles which had to be surmounted in a cost-effective manner. Supplied by reservoirs at **Winterburn, Foulridge, Barrowford** and **Rishton,** not unlike a necklace threading beads together, it acted as the communication link between villages and provided the crucial connection to the outside world. A whole new community came to life along the canals, sprawling along the banks, providing the flywheel for change and leaving behind, today, some of the finest industrial heritage in Great Britain.

The Weavers' Triangle Centre in Burnley straddles the Leeds/Liverpool Canal and shows the housing and buildings associated with the Industrial Revolution. Within a very short distance of these smoky mills are what is regarded as some of Britain's finest **canal bank scenery,** overlooked by Pendle and the upland of the Yorkshire Dales.

A STRETCH OF THE CANAL AT BURNLEY called the '**straight mile**' is classed as one of the seven wonders of Britain's waterways. It has an exhilarating embankment which looks down nearly 20 metres (60 ft) onto the town. Also at Burnley is the 511 metre (559 yard) long **Gannow Tunnel** and the **Yorkshire Street** '**Culvert**' which because of engineering difficulties was one of the most difficult and costly to construct. The locks at Barrowford are well worth seeing, while between **Barrowford** and **Barnoldswick** is the 1,500 metre (1,640 yard) long **Foulridge Tunnel,** (also known as Mile Tunnel) the longest in the County, which boasts a staggering story. In 1912 a cow fell into the water and by some miracle managed to swim right through the tunnel. This feat is remembered in pictures at the nearby **Hole in the Wall** public house.

THE DECLINE OF THE CANALS all over the country was due to the development of other forms of transport and problems with an increasingly unreliable water supply. Today, however, the **Canal** is being put to good use for recreational purposes, with boat hire and canal trips experiencing a rapid growth in popularity. Burnley Tourist Information Centre has a leaflet exploring the canal stretch from Wigan to Skipton.

The birth of the steam engine in the mid C19th was the catalyst for the final collapse of the canal system until, in the C20th, many canals became virtually derelict. Although the steam engine was more costly, it proved much more reliable and flexible than water power.

A RELIC OF THE AGE OF STEAM and a newcomer to Lancashire's Hill Country attractions is the **East Lancashire Railway**, run by the East Lancashire Railway Preservation Society. The line begins at **Bury**, passes through **Summerseat, Ramsbottom** and **Rawtenstall** and operates at weekends all year. There are also many special annual events. It links a multitude of attractions and leisure opportunities in the valley. The line was officially opened on April 27th 1991 and gave rise to many festive celebrations. The line has brought many towns and villages back into the age of the steam 'invasion', such as **Rawtenstall**, and lies in the heart of the **Irwell Valley**, an all year round tourism experience.

Dating from Georgian times is **Eanam Wharf**, a former canalside warehouse on the Leeds and Liverpool Canal, less than five minutes' walk from the town centre. Now renovated and acting as Blackburn's Business Development Centre, Eanam Wharf also houses a small **Visitor Centre** with a permanent exhibition on the canal heritage and an information point. The Visitor Centre provides a full range of educational activities. Eanam Wharf is at the centre of Blackburn waterside, the canal zone of Blackburn which is now an interesting visitor destination offering both recreational and shopping facilities. The towpath is a level, easy walk between venues and provides interesting views of the town. Details of canal boat trips can be had on request.

Annual Events & Customs

Lancashire's Hill Country offers a multitude of interesting traditional shows and annual events, so that at any given time throughout the year you will find a choice of experiences. There is only space to list a selection below but complete information may be obtained from the local **Tourist Information Centres**.

WELCOMING IN THE NEW YEAR consists of such traditions as ensuring that all outstanding bills are paid, household commodities are plentiful and that it is a young man with dark hair who is first to cross the doorstep, otherwise bad luck is liable to prevail. In an energetic beginning to the year, the areas of **Pendle** and **Rossendale** hold their annual sporting events on January 1st.

IN MARCH many wild flowers start to colour the countryside, and lambing commences in the lower dales towards the end of the month. **Simnel Sunday** is a traditional date on which spicy cakes are baked, following an old recipe which can be traced back to the 1780s. Of a more humorous nature, the farming community of **Longridge** and **Beacon Fell** celebrate **Shrovetide** by installing the last person to clear their plate in a wheelbarrow and depositing them on the nearest compost heap!

A magnificent vintage car at Towneley Hall near Burnley

DURING EASTER children are still known to take baskets or pillowcases from door to door asking for pancakes. These are not filled with pancakes, however, but oranges. In conjunction with these old customs, this is also the time of year when football mania intensifies. With the notable arrival of the cuckoo, April is rich in events ranging from the customary fooling on the 1st of the month to **Point to Point** meetings. **Good Friday** is celebrated with the beginning of the rambling and hill climbing year.

Eastertide also brings the **Ribble Valley Drama Festival**, held in Clitheroe and the arrival of the **Britannia Coconut Dancers**. The route takes the dancers from Britannia through Bacup to Stacksteads. Believed to have originated from Morocco around the C17th or C18th, they perform a ceremonial dance, evocative of an African tribal dance, with the emphasis on pagan rites and the dismissal of evil by whipping. Some believe the dancers also to have links with Cornish tin miners. Only a descendant of a 'coconutter' may become a dancer.

ON THE 12TH OF MAY winter is officially over and **maypole dancers** can still be seen on the streets of Burnley, also the host for the **National Blues Festival** and **Charity Horse Show**. Of a more typically local nature is the **Clitheroe Town Criers Competition**, which is open to the public and well worth an attempt. Meanwhile, May Bank Holiday sees the **Tour of Lancashire Cycle Race** pass through Lancashire's Hill Country.

THE SUMMER SEASON sees the majority of the historic houses open to the public, with June being the month for **Agricultural Shows** and the **Classic Car** and **Youth Band Contests**. **Bacup Carnival** is held every June. July is brimming with **Agricultural Shows** of interest to many people besides farmers, not least for the fine displays of **rural crafts**. There is also the annual judgement of the **Best Kept Village**, a major event for the local residents, with each location apprehensive of the outcome. **Rossfest** is held every Bank Holiday weekend.

THE MONTH OF AUGUST sees such events as the **Festival of Traditional Song and Dance** in **Burnley**, and yet more Agricultural Shows in **Longridge** and **Chipping**. It is also the month of **Haslingden Street Fair**. As the nights draw in, September sees the arrival of the **Hodder Valley Show**, while the infamous **Pendle Witches** prevail on the night of **Halloween**. With hunting now in full swing, November contains one of the more extraordinary customs, **Salmon Sunday**. On the closest Sunday to November 20th, people assemble in the Trough of Bowland at **Paythorne Bridge** to witness the coming of the salmon. Traditional **Christmas** celebrations then bring the year to a close.

Farming Past & Present

Despite its long history of the constant struggle to combat the elements, farming is still one of the primary and most productive industries in Lancashire's Hill Country today. Predominantly managed by family units, the farms, with a mean size of 36 hectares (89 acres), are comparatively humble in comparison to the average size of farms in England and Wales, which is 72 hectares (178 acres).

Farming, for so long the mainstay of the local population, has had an extensive impact on the rural landscape of Lancashire. This momentous transformation commenced when **Neolithic man** introduced Lancashire's Hill Country to the benefits of agriculture.

THE FIRST PIONEERS tended to avoid the hazardous valley bottoms and began their livelihood on the bleak hilltops. Subsequently, the clearance of trees and depletion of the surrounding soil forced the farmers to abandon their dwellings and proceed to a more fruitful location. This process tended to cause soil erosion and the resulting poor quality land was left waste. Crop yields were low and technical improvements were therefore greatly needed. This demand was met by the arrival of the **Romans**, who provided a sound road system and equipment to clear and cultivate suitable land.

Agriculture soon became man's main occupation and the growth of agriculture resulted in a dwindling of forests, and a need for **enclosed land** and **transport** like the Leeds and Liverpool Canal. These imparted to the landscape a striking change of appearance.

THE BOOM IN THE TEXTILE INDUSTRY led to good fortune for the farmers and families who were in great need of financial support due to widespread poverty caused by the fragmentation of farms. With a substantial population increase towards the end of the 1700s, the farming system moved from providing the farmer's own household with the bare necessities of life to dairy production for a rapidly increasing industrial population, and hence the necessity of a dual or supplementary income declined.

FURTHER AGRICULTURAL ADVANCEMENTS around the 1840s resulted in yet another transformation. The majority of suitable land, once used for **sheep** due to the expansion of the woollen industry, was then brought into use for the grazing of **cattle** and the production of hay, and therefore the sheep were relegated to the less fertile upland.

Today, the farms of Lancashire's Hill Country trade in a variety of commodities including milk, beef, barley, wheat and vegetables, but the most recent newcomer is probably the oil seed rape, whose colour-intense fields have transformed the rural landscape.

The pretty rural village of Dunsop Bridge

PARTIALLY DUE TO THE EEC, who changed the objectives of farming from production subsidies to a new emphasis on **conservation**, woodland on the farms has increased in the last decade by a third, and there has been a noticeable addition to ponds and wildlife habitats.

It is due to these changes and other contributing factors that only a minority of the families can now survive on the farm as a sole occupation. Many now have an **alternative source** of income derived from such activities as milk rounds and offering bed and breakfast accommodation.

A less welcome consequence of modernisation and the contraction of farming as a local industry is the increase of derelict land which has been abandoned for the more fruitful, but the agricultural landscape of Lancashire's Hill Country nevertheless remains one of the area's chief delights.

Local Legends & Dialect

POPULAR MYTHS AND LEGENDS, passed from generation to generation, cover almost every acre of the Hill Country. Records of **ghosts** stem from as far back as the second century BC, but although the district is largely identified with **witchcraft**, it is also renowned for its association with the **Devil** himself. It is believed that a considerable hole in the keep of **Clitheroe Castle** was caused by Satan hurling stones from the summit of **Pendle Hill**. Terrifying the streets of Clitheroe, he misled various youngsters into selling their souls in return for three wishes. One of the unfortunate was a **Nicholas Gosforth**, a tailor from Clitheroe, who later outwitted the Prince of Darkness and caused countless people to be filled with admiration.

Satan also made an appearance at the **Old Grammar School** in **Burnley**. Summoned by naïve schoolboys, he emerged from a flagstone, only to be hit over the head by the panic-stricken lads. From that day to this he has never been seen again in Burnley but there is a curious black mark on the aforementioned flagstone. Are you still sceptical?

Another dwelling connected with strange happenings is **Turton Tower** near **Darwen**. Haunting the tower is a lady, dressed in black and believed to be linked with illegal religious practices. There have been reports of noises and moving objects, believed to stem from the **Timberbottom skulls** here, that caused disturbances after their discovery in 1751.

BOGGARTS are common subject matter for tales concerning their mischievous antics. Hunting for pleasant shelter, these tiny, hard featured men, recompense the homeowner by inconspicuously helping around the home. If, however, their good deeds are acknowledged or they are seen in action, then begins the vexation.

One such location is **Towneley Hall, Burnley**. Plagued by the impertinent Boggart, the priest of Towneley was ordered to perform an exorcism on the dreadful creature. The Boggart agreed on the condition that a life was to be sacrificed to him every year. For the prevention of future disturbances, it became a custom on Boggarts Day to sacrifice the life of a chicken. The Boggart was never seen again.

OTHER STRANGE TALES include footsteps, chanting and the slamming of doors at **Whalley Abbey**, close to Clitheroe, and a horse rider known as **Ned King**, haunting **Hurst Green**. Of a more macabre nature, is the wicked and immoral **'headless woman'** who haunts the roads encircling **Longridge**. Terrorising the area, her head which was kept in a basket would chase her victims for some distance, its disconcerting laughter to be heard for miles around.

HILL COUNTRY'S DIALECT offers another rich field of exploration. The forthright patterns of speech and the colourful use of words, some tracing their origins back to other languages, such as **Scandinavian (Norse)**, **Gaelic** or **Latin**, give the several Lancashire dialects especial charm and interest. The origins of some words, such as **'dollop'**, meaning a shapeless lump, for instance, have never been traced.

The imposing style of Turton Tower

HILL COUNTRY PEOPLE are shrewd when managing their own affairs, as is illustrated by the many who are self-made and now wealthy; but they are also strikingly friendly and anyone visiting this area will be pleasantly surprised by the willingness of total strangers to stop, uninvited, and offer help if they think you need it. Listen, unobtrusively, to local speakers, and you will surely enjoy the variety injected into the English language by such dialects and come to hope that Joseph Wright's prediction, in 1904, of dialect dying out, will never come to fruition.

Outdoor Activities

For information about all outdoor sporting and leisure activities, call at Tourist Information Centres in the area for leaflets in the **'Lancashire's Great Outdoors'** series, published by **Lancashire County Council**. These include leaflets on **Adventure Sports**, **Horse Riding** and **Watersports**.

Sailing at Jumbles Country Park at Turton

LANCASHIRE'S HILL COUNTRY is considered **one of the best walking spots in Britain** and is known for its wealth of magnificent scenery, fell-top panoramas, sonorous rivers and beautiful woodlands.

Accompanied by detailed booklets and leaflets which are sold in many outlets, the walker in Hill Country is offered a host of differing walks for all ages. For the more experienced walker for example, there are the **Pennine Way** and the **Rossendale Way**, or for a more leisurely family walk there is the **Ribble Way** which follows a parallel course to the River Ribble, or the **Brontë Way** which pinpoints places of interest connected with the famous Brontë sisters.

Indeed Lancashire's Hill Country, believed to be the birthplace of walking for pleasure due to the smoky Industrial Revolution, has something to offer every enthusiastic walker, be it to witness the numerous viewpoints or just to fill your lungs with Lancashire fresh air.

If walking is not your preference then why not explore by **bicycle**? There are a number of trails which have been planned especially for the cyclist which will take you through some of the glorious countryside. So why not hire a bicycle and undertake the challenge of the 130 mile (208 km) trail which encompasses the area of Bowland?

For the more sporty visitors, Lancashire's Hill Country provides a magnitude of possibilities ranging from **Ski Rossendale**, a **dry ski-slope** near **Rawtenstall**, one of the largest in England, to **Waves Water Fun Centre** in **Blackburn**, which attracts over a quarter of a million people each year. If these do not appeal to you then maybe you might like to try **windsurfing, pony-trekking, hang-gliding, cycling, swimming, bowling, sailing, fishing** or **playing golf**.

A tranquil scene at Barnoldswick boatyard

A LIST OF INDOOR SPORTS FACILITIES is available from Tourist Information Centres. It is entitled **'Lancashire's Great Indoors'** and is published by **Lancashire County Council**. The possibilities are almost limitless, so why not take the plunge and treat yourself to a great day out?

The Riches of Nature

The wildlife of Lancashire's Hill Country, vibrant and rich in variety, is the pride of local inhabitants, and the wealth of plants, trees, insects, birds and mammals have been protected for numerous years by the various County Councils who are devoted to the conservation of the area.

It has therefore been possible not only to maintain its natural beauty, but also to improve it to a certain extent. **Country Parks** and **Nature Reserves** offer a rich habitat for many creatures and provide a setting in which visitors can enjoy these aspects.

SOME OF THE MOST RENOWNED BIRD WATCHING SITES in the country are to be found here; for example **sparrow-hawks**, **kestrels** and various **owls** can be seen in their natural environment. The **Royal Society for the Protection of Birds** (RSPB) helps to ensure their welfare and preserve their natural habitat by limiting access for the public, as in the **Forest of Bowland**. Apart from the birds these areas are populated with a diversity of animals such as **rabbits, brown hares, foxes** and **deer**. Even sightings of the **Japanese Sika deer**, established in Britain in the C19th, have been recorded.

Maintenance of nature's food cycle is essential for wildlife, both animal and plant, to prosper. Wild flowers grace the landscape with their colour and beauty, typifying the perfect English country scene, but some species are endangered due to man's activity and should neither be picked nor dug up. Wild flowers are juxtaposed with much scrub and woodland.

Wildlife Sites to Visit

More information concerning all the following locations can be obtained from local **Tourist Information Centres** and the **Lancashire Trust for Nature Conservation** (LTNC).

BALLGROVE PICNIC SITE Cotton Tree, Colne. With sub-aqua diving, canoeing and coarse fishing, this conservation area has something to offer everyone, with a picnic and playground area for the less energetic.

BARLEY PICNIC SITE Barley, Nelson. Based near an Information Centre, which can provide many varied souvenirs and details of local history, the site attracts walkers from **Ogden Reservoir, Black Moss** and the famous **Pendle Hill**.

Open expanses of rich purple moorland on Longridge Fell

COWME RESERVOIR An attractive reservoir with a range of water sports available. Contact Cowme Valley Ski Club.

FOXHILL BANK NATURE RESERVE Located some 150 metres to the north-west of Union Road (B6231) Oswaldtwistle. Access to the site from Union Road via Badger Brow or Mill Hill. Situated in the valley of Timber Brook close to Oswaldtwistle town centre, this site which is managed by Lancashire Wildlife Trust contains a variety of wildlife habitats including two wetland areas (former reservoirs), grassland and a range of woodland.

HEALEY DELL NATURE RESERVE Off the A671 Bacup/Rochdale Road, Whitworth. Surrounded by outstanding woodland and housing a fabulous stone viaduct crossing the valley, there is much to see whilst on any of the Nature Trails provided by this Nature Reserve.

Quiet river habitat near Wycoller packhorse bridge

JACK HOUSE RESERVOIR AND THE HASLINGDEN GRANE Oswaldtwistle. There is a series of walks which accompany you around this area, designed by the local Civic Society.

MILL HILL PICNIC SITE Childers Green, Burnley. Mill Hill Picnic Site is situated next to a wood, with old castle remains in close proximity.

ROCKWATER BIRD CONSERVATION CENTRE Cliviger, Burnley.

RODDLESWORTH NATURE TRAIL This 1 mile (2 km) trail starts from Tockholes village near Darwen and passes the ruins of the C18th Hollinshead Hall. There is plenty of wildlife interest and some fine views to enjoy.

ROSSENDALE GROUNDWORK COUNTRY - SIDE CENTRE New Hall Hey Road, Rawtenstall. With a variety of attractions from a giant willow-tree sculpture to a farm centre and a herb garden, this centre has much to offer, with its guided walks and lovely picnic site. It is highly recommended for a wonderful day out.

ROWLEY LAKE Heasandford, Burnley. Surrounded by footpaths, this man-made lake is home to an abundance of water-fowl and is perfect for the avid fisherman, a beautiful place to take a picnic. There are toilets and parking facilities.

SPRING WOOD Whalley. Famed for its bluebells, this wood has picnic and car park facilities, with scenic walks through the woodland.

STOCKS RESERVOIR Located in the **Forest of Bowland** north of **Slaidburn** and surrounded by **Gisburn Forest**, Stocks Reservoir covers the remains of a village called **Dalehead**. Only when there is a severe shortage of water can parts of this underwater village be seen.

STUBBYLEE AND MOORLANDS PARKS Bacup. A guided tour brochure is available from the refreshment kiosk and there is plenty of interest for both adults and children (interpretive trail).

SUNNYHURST WOOD AND VISITOR CENTRE off Earnsdale Road, Darwen. Backed by the beautiful **Darwen Moors**, which offer a number of walks and nature trails, lies this marvellous Visitor Centre, with displays of art and local natural history.

THURSDEN PICNIC SITE Burnley. Surrounded by photogenic views of Thursden, this picnic area is the ideal place for that peaceful afternoon amidst beautiful scenery.

TOGDEN VALLEY Barley. There are guided walks and trails available, with parking and refreshments at the Visitors Centre.

WALVERDEN RESERVOIR Nelson. Created in 1869, the Reservoir now supplies the village of Nelson with an abundant water supply and offers a range of recreational activities from bird-watching to guided walks.

WITTON COUNTRY PARK AND VISITOR CENTRE Preston Old Road, Blackburn. With nearly 200 hectares (480 acres) of fabulous farm and woodland there is plenty to occupy the visitor here. There are farm equipment exhibits, a small mammal centre, many interesting and varied trails showing the differing landscapes and habitats, and Dusty the horse to fill your day. There is also a popular Outdoor Leisure Centre.

WYCOLLER COUNTRY PARK Wycoller, Colne. With some remains dating from between 3,000 and 1,000 years BC, Wycoller Country Park is a conservation area, consisting of ancient bridges and the remains of an old hall which has strong Brontë connections.

Historic Buildings

For information about opening times please contact local Tourist Information Centres.

Castles, Halls & Abbey Ruins

BROWSHOLME HALL Bashall Eaves, Nr Clitheroe. Restricted opening. Home of the **Parker family** since the C14th, this English country mansion built in 1509 is situated in beautiful surroundings and houses family portraits by Deuws, Romney, Batoni and Worthcote, fine original furniture, oak panelling and many family treasures. Of a more curious nature, it was believed that the skull of a martyr once housed in the family chapel, when buried as a practical joke in the garden by **Edward Parker**, caused fires to break out with no logical explanation, numerous family deaths, and the facade of the house to fall away. Fear which struck the family forced Edward to own up to his boyish prank and after the skull was returned, everything was back to normal. With much to offer and explore, Browsholme Hall is well worth a visit.

CLITHEROE CASTLE Castle Hill, Clitheroe. Standing in capacious grounds, Clitheroe Castle, once the home of the **de Lacy family**, commands panoramic views of the Bowland Fells, Pendle Hill and the Ribble Valley. The Castle has one of the oldest and smallest Norman keeps in the country and also boasts a beautiful rose garden planted in honour of George VI's Coronation in 1937. Of a more fictitious nature, it is believed that Satan has a strong connection with a mysterious hole in the wall of the Castle's keep, reputedly caused by the Devil himself continually throwing stones from the summit of Pendle Hill! See also Clitheroe Museum.

GAWTHORPE HALL Padiham, Nr Burnley. Believed to have been originally designed by **Robert Smythson** between 1600 and 1605, this Jacobean manor house was remodelled in the C17th by **Sir Charles Barry**, who restored the Hall to its Victorian character. Gawthorpe Hall, surrounded by splendid countryside and owned by the National Trust since 1972, contains the famous **Rachel Kay Shuttleworth Needlework collection**, paintings from the National Portrait Gallery ranging from the C17th and C18th, and also Ryder furniture from England and Europe. The Hall also offers a shop and an entertainments centre, an attractive and interesting place for all the family to visit.

HOGHTON TOWER Situated above the River Darwen, this C16th mansion stands where the homes of the **de Hoghton family** have been sited since the C11th. The actual tower which was once part of this impressive mansion was destroyed by the Roundheads in 1643. None the less there are still many magnificent rooms to be seen. The Banqueting Hall tells of James I in 1617 knighting a loin of beef **'Sir Loin'** and how **William Shakespeare** performed for the de Hoghton family. As a contrast to this there is an Old English Rose Garden surrounded by breathtaking scenery to enjoy.

The imposing gatehouse of Hoghton Tower

SAMLESBURY HALL Preston New Road, Samlesbury. This half-timbered, medieval house has a **Great Hall, Long Gallery** and an **archery field** supposed to have been in regular use ever since the C14th.

SAWLEY ABBEY Sawley, Nr Clitheroe. Sawley Abbey, of Cistercian ancestry, was founded in 1147 by the third **Baron de Percy,** and lies on the banks of the River Ribble.

STONYHURST COLLEGE Near Hurst Green. Built around 1523 by Hugh Shireburn, Stonyhurst College resides on the edge of the Longridge Fells, and for the past two hundred years has housed a famed boarding school for boys of the Roman Catholic faith. Many interesting and valuable items are on display. Many additions have been made to this impressive building throughout the years but its original architectural beauty still remains.

TURTON TOWER Chapeltown, Nr Bromley. Sited in wooded countryside which stretches for 3.6 hectares (9 acres), this C12th half-timbered Tudor house was once the home of **Humphrey Chetham,** the Sheriff of Lancashire, and formerly treasurer of the Roundheads. The

Chetham family resided at this address until 1835 when **James Kay** bought it and restored the Tower to its former glory. In the early 1900s the **Knowles family** donated the Tower to the Turton Urban District Council and it is now open to the public with displays of old armour, weapons and a marvellous selection of C17th furniture.

WHALLEY ABBEY South of Clitheroe. Situated on the banks of the River Calder, discovered by the **Cistercians** in 1296, Whalley Abbey is surrounded by panoramic scenery. Whispered tales have been told of footsteps and singing, shutting doors and the figures of nuns and monks prowling around the premises. Why not take a guided tour and discover its remains?

Churches & Cathedrals

BLACKBURN CATHEDRAL Blackburn. The foundations of Blackburn Cathedral have been occupied since before the C6th and it is the remains of the 1896 Church which is now the nave of the more modern Anglican Cathedral, the only one in Lancashire. There is a worthy collection of art treasures and a tablet of the crucifixion within.

The evocative ruins of Sawley Abbey

GOODSHAW OLD BAPTIST CHAPEL Rossendale. Built in the C18th, this attractive old Chapel has been renovated by English Heritage and is now considered one of the most beautiful Non-Conformist buildings. Take a walk around the graveyard and pursue the fascinating inscriptions on a multitude of gravestones.

PARISH CHURCH OF ST MARY Newchurch in Pendle. Formerly a Chapel of Ease dating from the C15th. The church tower supports what is known as the 'Eye of God' which was supposed to protect people from evil.

SACRED HEART ROMAN CATHOLIC CHURCH Colne. An outstanding **mosaic interior** was designed in Italy and brought to Colne in transportable sections to decorate this Roman Catholic church

An unusual and interesting view of Whalley Abbey

SOUTHFIELD METHODIST CHURCH Nelson. Memorabilia of **John Wesley,** who preached at Southfield in 1786, after the Methodists had made it their regular meeting place, are to be found recorded on the exterior wall of this chapel.

ST BARTHOLOMEW'S CHURCH Colne. The conventional ancient custom was for a church to lie east to west, but St Bartholomew's Church, built in 1122 and thus the oldest building in Pendle, was sited for the east side to face the geographical spot where the sun rises on the Patron Saint's day.

ST JAMES CHURCH Accrington. Built in 1763 and enlarged and altered at various dates in the early C19th. This church displays a number of wall tablets, principally to members of the Peel and Hargreaves families.

ST JOSEPH'S ROMAN CATHOLIC CHURCH Nelson. Tragically, in 1960, this Church was burnt to the ground after only sixty-three years of existence. Taking a period of four years, a new Church was built in its ashes which many think to be breathtaking in its simplicity.

ST MARY LE GHYLL CHURCH Barnoldswick. This Church houses a memorable **three-tier pulpit** dating from the C17th.

ST PAUL'S Little Marsden. At the west end of this C13th Church are the **'Singing Pews'** and the **gallery,** which are of particular interest.

ST PETER'S CHURCH Burnley. The origins of St Peter's go back to 1122 and the Church is considered to mark Burnley's historical centre.

Museums & Galleries

ASTLEY HALL MUSEUM AND ART GALLERY Astley Park, Chorley. Though just outside Lancashire's Hill Country, this important museum deserves mention here. Originally built around 1580, the three-storey Elizabethan Hall was an impressive English Renaissance building which, when rebuilt in 1666, took on a Jacobean style. Standing in wooded parkland the Hall offers many recreational activities from bowling, nature trails and picnic areas to a children's playground. Inside the Hall are many items of interest, ranging from the great **'Sirloin' chair** which was once used by **James I** when he knighted the loin of beef at **Hoghton Tower**, to an Elizabethan bed which is locally known as the **Cromwell Bed**, due to a well recalled visit. The **Art Gallery** offers a variety of exhibitions which include paintings, Leeds pottery, horse brasses, lead soldiers and some of Oliver Cromwell's attire.

BACUP NATURAL HISTORY MUSEUM Yorkshire Street, Bacup. Restricted opening. The Museum is housed in an elegant C18th building which displays photography, industrial, natural and fascinating social history.

BANCROFT MILL ENGINE MUSEUM Bancroft Shed, Gillians Lane, Barnoldswick. This exhibition relates to the weaving industry, with tools, machines and documents all on display. There is a demonstration of the only **working steam engine** left in the area which once lived in Barnoldswick. After the Mill's closure in 1978 the engine was restored and rehoused for all to see. A recent addition is a traditional **Lancashire loom** which is demonstrated in all its splendour on a regular basis.

BLACKBURN MUSEUM AND ART GALLERY Museum Street, Blackburn. With a collection of a thousand **Japanese prints**, eight works by **J.M.W. Turner, Egyptian artifacts**, the **Hart Collection** of medieval manuscripts and coins, the Museum houses a wide variety of fascinating collections. Other attractions include the **East Lancashire Regiment Gallery** and a major feature on **Asian culture** which is displayed in its own dedicated gallery.

BRITISH IN INDIA MUSEUM Newtown Street, Colne. In a museum founded in 1972, this striking exhibition covers memorabilia from the British in India to the Independence in 1947. Telling the story of the **British Raj**, it offers paintings, photographs, medals, model soldiers, letters, military uniforms and the not-to-be-missed model of the Kalka Simla Railway, which is in splendid working order.

BURNLEY MECHANICS Manchester Road, Burnley. Opened in the autumn of 1986 and presenting an all-year-round programme with major annual events, the Burnley Mechanics Arts and Entertainments Centre provides a variety of entertainment ranging from classical, jazz and blues music, to participation in dance, crafts and drama. It is also the home of Burnley TIC.

CLITHEROE CASTLE MUSEUM Castle Hill, Clitheroe. The Castle Museum relates the history of Clitheroe and its surrounding areas, both in the displays and by means of a new sound system. A new addition of the **Geology Room** has much to offer.

EARBY LEAD MINES MUSEUM The Old Grammar School, School Lane, Earby. This is a small museum in an early C17th Grammar School. It concentrates on the **C19th lead mining in the Yorkshire Dales**, showing a variety of mining equipment, a mineral collection and many working models.

Helmshore Textile and Higher Mill Museums

EAST LANCASHIRE RAILWAY Rawtenstall. For details of this 'living' museum see the chapter 'Canals and Railways'.

GALLERY DOWNSTAIRS Mid-Pennine Arts Association, Yorke Street, Burnley. Rotating on a five week period, the museum exhibits contemporary, professional and mixed media visual arts.

HAWORTH ART GALLERY Haworth Park, Manchester Road, Accrington. Situated in superb parkland, this is considered to be one of the most attractive museums in Britain, containing a fabulous **Tiffany glass collection** and a number of exquisite paintings counterbalanced by visiting exhibitions.

HELMSHORE TEXTILE MUSEUMS Holcolmbe Road, Helmshore, Rossendale. Powered by water, this C18th woollen fulling mill, built in

1789 by the **Turner family**, houses Arkwright's inventions including the famous **Water Twist Frame**. These are regularly displayed and demonstrated. As an interesting comparison there is also an updated version of James Hargreaves' **'Spinning Jenny'**.

The appealing exterior of Pendle Heritage Centre

LEWIS TEXTILE MUSEUM Exchange Street, Blackburn. This Museum commemorates the transition of the cotton industry from manual to machine-powered spinning and weaving, which in turn, transformed the area both in terms of landscape and social life. The memorable machines which brought fame to **Crompton, Arkwright, Hargreaves** and **Kay** can be seen in their working splendour, with regular art exhibitions in the upstairs gallery.

MOTORCYCLE MUSEUM Winfields, Hazel Hill, Blackburn Road, Haslingden. Steve McQueen's 1937 498cc **Scott Flying Squirrel motorcycle**, complete with side-car, is one of the main attractions of the Museum, with exhibits which range from the 1930s to the modern day - a must for those who long for the days when bike touring was a real possibility.

MUSEUM OF CHILDHOOD 33 Church Street, Ribchester. With fifty-four dolls houses, toys and models, a Professor Tomlin's Flea Circus and a model fairground in working order, this Museum has many delights to offer, with occasional **Punch and Judy shows** to keep the younger generation amused whilst you take time to discover an unbelievable variety of exhibits.

MUSEUM OF ROMAN ANTIQUITIES Riverside, Ribchester. Set beside the lovely Ribble River, on the site of an old Roman fort, is a fascinating display of Roman antiquities which include the renowned **Ribchester helmet**, Roman inscriptions and much more.

NORTH WEST SOUND ARCHIVE Old Steward's Office, Clitheroe Castle, Clitheroe. Listen to the local dialect and the many Lancashire traditions, just a handful of over 85,000 sound recordings for you to enjoy.

PENDLE ANTIQUES CENTRE Union Mill, Wall Street, Sabden. During the season this Centre attracts more than five hundred visitors a week. This old cotton mill, now owned by Walter and Beryl Aspinall, houses many curios from jewellery to furniture. Also of interest is an exhibition of many historical exhibits with a friendly cafe to complete the visit.

PENDLE HERITAGE CENTRE Park Hill, Barrowford, Nelson. Associated with the **Bannister family** (Roger Bannister was the first man to run a mile in under four minutes), this C17th historic house tells of the local textile industry, the people and the buildings. Also of interest is a **Pendle Witches display**, telling of the whispered tales and the curious events which are still remembered today. For those who enjoy the outdoors there is also an C18th **walled garden** to enjoy and a C15th **cruck barn** with rare breeds and other livestock.

PENDLE PHOTOGRAPHIC GALLERY Town Hall, Market Street, Nelson. You cannot fail to be captivated by this exhibition of photography and art which keeps your attention by an almost magical transition from subject to subject.

The Museum of Roman Antiquities at Ribchester

PENDLE TOY AND TRAIN MUSEUM Watt Street, Sabden, Nr Padiham. Here an extensive exhibition of model trains, boats, cars and toys, includes examples from many years ago to the present day.

PENNINE AVIATION MUSEUM Moorlands Park, Bacup. Viewing by appointment only. A range of aviation exhibits can be seen including a Canberra TT8, a De Havilland Vampire and an Avro Anson Mk. 21

QUEEN STREET MILL Harle Syke, Burnley. Here you will be able to witness the sights and sounds of a Lancashire weaving mill and discover authentic factory conditions in this, the **only remaining steam-powered cotton mill in Britain.** It was rebuilt in 1894 during the time when Burnley was in the heart of the Industrial Revolution. The 500hp steam engine **'Peace'** drives over two hundred looms which are working to produce saleable items in the shop, along with others of its kind, by staff dressed in the 1890s regalia. With a little imagination you will feel as though you are back a hundred years in time. Re-opening date summer 1994.

The Groundwork Countryside Centre at Rawtenstall

ROSSENDALE FOOTWEAR HERITAGE MUSEUM Gaghills Mill, off Burnley Road East, Waterfoot. Occupying the site of a C19th **Trickett's Gaghills Mill,** this Museum which opened in spring 1991 has a display of footwear manufacture ranging from the 1870s to the present day.

ROSSENDALE MUSEUM Whitaker Park, Haslingden Road, Rawtenstall. Built in 1840 by a member of the **Hardman family** and opened in 1902, this Victorian mansion house once called Oak Hill, lies in the vast grounds of **Whitaker Park,** overlooking a **Hardman woollen mill** at **New Hall Hey,** the focus of the excellent Groundwork Countryside Centre (see 'The Riches of Nature'). Displays include furniture, local and natural history, ceramics, taxidermy, costume and footwear and fine art - or maybe you could discover the portraits of the **Whitehead family,** who took over the park in 1900.

STEAM MUSEUM Tabber Caravan Park, Gisburn, Clitheroe. The museum contains many rare, renovated steam engines, which include what is believed to be the only known **Howard, Porter and early Aveling Traction Engines** as well as a unique **Foster steam wagon.** Another must for all you steam enthusiasts!

Towneley Hall Art Gallery and Museum at Burnley

TOWNELEY HALL ART GALLERY AND MUSEUM Towneley Park, Burnley. Originating in the C14th and formerly the home of the Towneley family for more than five hundred years, Towneley Hall was converted into a fine Museum for all to enjoy its splendour in 1902. Set in vast acres of parkland, the historic house contains many C18th and C19th paintings, individual rooms furnished with C14th furniture, **Pilkington Royal Lancashire Pottery,** archaeology and local history. The Museum grounds offer nature trails, golf, bowling, tennis and a more recent addition, an aquarium.

WEAVERS' COTTAGE Fall Barn, Rawtenstall. Aspects from the working conditions, local history, social life and the architecture of the woollen industry are exhibited in this well preserved, C18th former loom shop.

WEAVERS' TRIANGLE VISITORS CENTRE 85 Manchester Road, Burnley. With a collection of buildings dating from the Industrial Revolution, the Centre straddles the **Leeds/Liverpool Canal** and is considered to be one of the best preserved industrial landscapes in Lancashire. Run by volunteers, there are displays featuring the social life of the weavers, a model fairground and an exhibition covering the development of the Weavers' Triangle.

WYCOLLER CRAFT CENTRE Wycoller Country Park, Wycoller, Colne. Characteristic of Victorian times, the Centre offers the opportunity to purchase a variety of items, including local crafts, leather goods, hand-made toys, decorated eggs and Pendle Witches memorabilia.

Towns & Villages of the Area

Half day closing in Lancashire's Hill Country is as follows:
Tuesday - Bacup, Burnley, Colne, Darwen, Padiham, Nelson and Rawtenstall.
Wednesday - Accrington, Clitheroe and Haslingden.
Thursday - Blackburn.
Many shops are renouncing the half day closing tradition but it is as well to check before your departure.

The area abounds with opportunities for those seeking a bargain in one of the many local markets. Some of the markets have been held continuously since the C13th and today they are a really enjoyable traditional aspect of life in Lancashire's Hill Country. These occur on the following days:
Nelson - Wednesday, Friday and Saturday.
Colne - Wednesday and Saturday.
Burnley - Monday, Wednesday (for the bric à brac), Thursday and Saturday.
Clitheroe - Tuesday and Saturday.
Accrington - Tuesday, Friday and Saturday.
Rawtenstall - Thursday and Saturday.
Blackburn - Wednesday, Friday and Saturday.
Darwen - Monday, Friday and Saturday.
Padiham - Wednesday, Friday and Saturday (for antiques and bric à brac).
Bacup - Wednesday and Saturday.

ACCRINGTON (Hyndburn) Accrington, once a cotton manufacturing town of Saxon origins, matured quickly during the Industrial Revolution but still retains its Victorian characteristics. Overlooked by the marvellous **Accrington Viaduct**, the town centre has been appointed as an 'Outstanding Conservation Area'. The town is probably best known for its red engineering bricks, known as the '**Accrington Bloods**', and of course for **Accrington Stanley**, the founding member of the Football League.

BACUP (Rossendale) Bacup is the home of the **Britannia Coconut Dancers** and was once associated with the textile industry. Enclosed by moorland, Bacup is an 'Urban Conservation Area'.

BARNOLDSWICK (Colne) This small town, with its attractive cobbled square, has its origins in Saxon times but developed with the coming of the Leeds and Liverpool Canal and the growth of the textile industry. Barnoldswick is surrounded by rolling hills, offering outstanding views over Yorkshire's limestone country. A Town Trail Leaflet is available.

BLACKBURN (Blackburn) A city whose history can be traced from over a thousand years ago, which includes a mention in the Domesday Book, Blackburn began as a farming community but, being at the core of the Industrial Revolution, it became actively involved in the weaving industry. **Hargreaves**, the inventor of the '**Spinning Jenny**', was born here but his invention did not immediately catch on. The influence of both the 'Spinning Jenny' and the Dandy Loom can be seen on the dome of **St John's Church** where the shape of a weaving shuttle is used as a weather vane. Blackburn's prosperity is also seen in its many other fine Victorian buildings, and its **Imperial Mill**, built in 1901 and still standing, was once the largest spinning mill in the world. The town boasts the magnificent **Ewood Aqueduct** and also the finest **railway station** in Lancashire. For a note on **Blackburn Cathedral** see the chapter on 'Historic Buildings'. **Blackburn Museum and Art Gallery** and the **Lewis Textile Museum** are both featured under 'Museums and Galleries'.

BOLTON-BY-BOWLAND (Ribble Valley) This scenic, tranquil village boasts two village greens, the smaller of which contains the remains of a C13th market cross and stocks. The second lies above the C13th **Church of St Peter and St Paul** where a wealthy land owner, **Sir Ralph Pudsey**, rests in peace with his three wives and twenty-five children. It is said that in 1464 Sir Ralph sheltered King Henry VI fleeing from his enemies.

BURNLEY (Burnley) First established around 800 AD, between the Rivers Calder and the Brun, Burnley covers an area of some 50 square miles (130 sq kms) which houses an abundance of variety. The world's former leading producer of cotton cloth is enhanced by magnificent countryside, attractive historic houses and some of the best preserved industrial landscapes and architecture, such as the **Burnley Viaduct** which carries the Leeds to Liverpool Canal through the town centre. See the chapter 'Museums and Galleries' for further details of Burnley's many interesting places to visit.

CHAPELTOWN south of Darwen (Blackburn). This pretty moorland village has plenty of interesting buildings dating back as early as Tudor times.

CHIPPING (Ribble Valley) Situated in beautiful countryside, Chipping, once a market town, contains stone built houses and cobbled pavements. During the Industrial Revolution Chipping became a fruitful centre for the wool trade and flax spinning. Many of the C17th buildings are left as an apt reminder of the days gone by. From a bridge in Talbot Street, one can capture views of fantastic beauty. Looking downstream towards the crest of Longridge Fell, one sees an old mill complete with old water wheel, which once produced the power needed for the function of the mill. Well worth a visit is the **village Church** which is commemorated by an annual fair held on St Bartholomew's Day, August 24th.

CLAYTON-LE-MOORS (Hyndburn) Situated between Accrington and Great Harwood, Clayton-Le-Moors originated from the villages of Enfield and Oakenshaw and in years gone by was known as the 'clay town in the moors'. Famed for its production of the 'Dr Lovelace' soap and calico printing, this town proves well worth a visit.

CLITHEROE (Ribble Valley) This charming, bustling market town, which has recently celebrated its 800th birthday, is situated in the Ribble Valley and is well known for its natural beauty. Dominating the town is the C12th **Norman Castle**, an ideal place from which to view the streets of Clitheroe and the distant fells. Many will be familiar with the family owned wine shop called D. Byrne and Company which has appeared in the 'Which' wine guide and one must pay a visit to the Cowman's sausage shop, which has an outstanding variety of tasty sausages.

COLNE (Pendle) is believed to originate from Roman times, but is probably better known for its active part in the weaving and textile industry, the centrepiece of which was a building called Cloth Hall, now demolished. Colne was the birth town of the well-known jam maker **Sir William Hartley**, and of a very brave **Wallace Hartley**, bandmaster on the Titanic, still remembered by a bust which can be seen near the War Memorial.

DARWEN (Blackburn) Darwen is famed for the commanding tower which stands high above the charming market town. Popular as a landmark for local walkers, Darwen Tower was built in 1898 to commemorate Queen Victoria's Diamond Jubilee. **India Mill** and **Moss Bridge Mill** both retain their old steam engines and are of interest to lovers of industrial archaeology.

DOWNHAM (Ribble Valley) This Elizabethan village, lying below the majestic **Pendle Hill**, has long been associated with the **Assheton family**. They made their mark by building **Downham Hall**, the **school, vicarage** and the **Church of St Leonard**. Their work produced a uniquely picturesque and atmospheric village and they will be remembered by many.

GISBURN (Ribble Valley) Gisburn is a village steeped in history, ancient cottages, houses and a **Church** to tell the tale.

GREAT HARWOOD (Hyndburn) Great Harwood is well known for mercerisation of cotton, a treatment of cotton fabric or thread to give greater strength. **John Mercer** was the commendable inventor who is honoured by a clock-tower in the town square. The village boasts beautiful, captivating views to the north.

GREAT MITTON (Ribble Valley) Situated south of Clitheroe, Great Mitton stands beside the sonorous River Ribble. Standing above is the C14th **Church of All Hallows**, picturesque in its beauty. Also of interest in this delightful village is an ornate Jacobean Hall.

HASLINGDEN (Rossendale) Surrounded by moorlands, Haslingden is famous for its stone flags which are exported throughout the world, including the paving of Trafalgar Square.

HOLME CHAPEL (Burnley) In the well kept village of Holme Chapel, there is an impressive record of Lady O'Hagen and Lady Scarlett who resided in the local **Towneley Hall**, aptly named after a family who lived there for over five hundred years. Towneley Hall is one of Lancashire's finest stately homes, set in beautiful parkland and now containing a superb Art Gallery and Museum. **General Scarlett**, a leader of the Heavy Brigade at Balaclava, is buried with many notable Burnley dwellers in the local church.

The quaint stone-built cottages of Downham near Clitheroe

HURST GREEN (Ribble Valley) This village is famed for its association with **Stonyhurst College**, one of the most notable boarding schools for boys of the Roman Catholic faith. With the Longridge Fells as its backdrop, Hurst Green is linked with the family name **Shireburn**, builders of the **Shireburn Almshouses** in 1706.

HURSTWOOD (Burnley) A very attractive and charming village, surrounded by breathtaking countryside and lying next to the River Brun. Amongst its best buildings are **Tattersall's House, Hurstwood Hall**, built by Barnard

Towneley in 1579, and **Spenser's Cottage,** the former home of the Elizabethan poet Edmund Spenser. **Three Reservoir Walks** can be enjoyed in the area.

LONGRIDGE (Ribble Valley) Longridge provides a vast shopping and social centre for farming folk from miles around. With majestic views of the Fylde Plane, **Longridge Fell** dominates a variety of superb views which include Ingleborough, Loud Valley, the Isle of Man and the Welsh mountains on a clear day.

LOW MOOR VILLAGE near Clitheroe (Ribble Valley). Lancashire's largest mill village, dating from 1800.

NELSON (Pendle) The origins of Nelson can be traced as far back as 1311 when there were two tiny farming settlements, then known as Great and Little Marsden, but it was a tribute to the great **Lord Nelson** which gave the town its new name. With an interesting mixture of traditional cottages and modern developments, Nelson now boasts an outdoor market.

NEWTON (Ribble Valley) Views of magnificent beauty are obtained from the top of **Waddington Fell,** near Newton, but probably the most breathtaking are to be viewed from the west overlooking the **Trough of Bowland.** This commanding old village is known for its strong connection with the Quaker Movement.

OSWALDTWISTLE (Hyndburn) Oswaldtwistle is renowned as the home of **James Hargreaves,** the inventor of the '**Spinning Jenny',** and the reformer **Robert 'Parsley' Peel.** Explore the abundance of footpaths contained within this notable village.

PADIHAM (Burnley) Lying approximately 4 miles (6 kms) from Burnley, Padiham has a history stretching back before the Norman Conquest. In the C20th there still remain many characteristics of the industrial past for curious visitors to discover.

RAWTENSTALL (Rossendale) Forming one of the three major towns of the Borough of Rossendale, Rawtenstall is steeped in history, with many once used mills and industrial buildings to tell its tale, including the last remaining traditional Herbalist/Temperance Bar in Britain. See the **Rossendale Museum** and **Weavers' Cottage,** both under 'Museums and Galleries' for further details. Backed by the wonderful hills which form the Pennines, Rawtenstall has much to offer. The **East Lancashire Railway** runs between Rawtenstall, Ramsbottom and Bury, where vintage steam trains run at weekends and Bank Holidays.

RIBCHESTER (Ribble Valley) Nestling by the River Ribble, and surrounded by lovely green hills, Ribchester has strong Roman connections, with a sizeable **Roman fort site,** built around 80 AD, to tell the tale. Remains of this fort can be seen in the local C13th **Church,** which commemorates St Christopher, the patron saint of travellers. For details of the **Museum of Roman Antiquities** see the 'Museums and Galleries' chapter.

SALTERFORTH (Pendle) This pretty village between Barnoldswick and Earby has won the 'Best Kept Village in Lancashire' award.

SAWLEY (Ribble Valley) Lying on the banks of the River Ribble, Sawley was named after a **Cistercian Abbey, Salley,** whose ruins lie alongside the winding Ribble.

SLAIDBURN (Ribble Valley) Set below the **Forest of Bowland,** this village, mainly built of grey stone, has an air of stability and wisdom. Its attractive Church's history can be traced back to the C12th. Moving on seven centuries, why not visit the local inn called '**Hark to Bounty',** named after a foxhound who barked constantly whenever his master was drinking in the inn, leading to the phrase 'Hark to Bounty'.

STYDD (Ribble Valley) Stydd, situated in the Ribble Valley, is famed for the **Almshouses** built in 1728 by the **Sherburnes** but another local attraction is a tiny C16th octagonal **Norman Church** founded by the Knights of St John, secluded in a nearby field.

TOCKHOLES (Blackburn). This unusually named village lies at the edge of **Darwen Moor,** overlooked by the **Jubliee Tower,** to which a footpath leads. There are many C17th weavers' cottages and farms.

WADDINGTON near Clitheroe (Ribble Valley). This is another regular winner of the title 'Best Kept Village in Lancashire'.

WHALLEY (Ribble Valley) Famed for its churches, Whalley's **St Mary's and All Saints Church** houses three C10th Celtic crosses in its churchyard with many antiquities held inside from **Whalley Abbey** which was founded in Norman times, now lying in ruins. There are many buildings from Georgian and Tudor times, with a cricket field which belonged to the Grammar School, where the first '**Roses' match** was held between Lancashire and Yorkshire. An impressive example of Victorian engineering skills is the red-brick **Whalley Viaduct.**

WORSTHORNE (Burnley) Intertwined with the **Thursby family** who were benefactors of the Burnley area, Worsthorne, a conservation area, has numerous listed buildings which include the **Church of St John the Evangelist** with an enchanting display of wrought ironwork.

WYCOLLER (Pendle) Wycoller, now a **Country Park and Conservation Area,** is a charming village with a stream running through its centre, under seven delightful and curious bridges. Its romantic and majestic quality so charmed **Charlotte Brontë** that she used the local Ferndean Manor in her novel 'Jane Eyre'.

Holden Clough Nursery

Set in the scenic Forest of Bowland, and situated in the pretty village of Holden, near Bolton-by-Bowland, **Holden Clough Nursery**, established in 1927, is a mecca for gardeners interested in **unusual alpines** and **hardy plants**.

The present owners, **Peter and Anne Foley**, have introduced many new and rare varieties to the Nursery, and also grow a comprehensive range of **ornamental grasses**, **heathers**, **ferns**, **dwarf conifers**, **shrubs** and **climbing plants**. Their specialities include **Astilbes**, **Primulas**, **Hostas** and **Saxifrages**, as well as a wide range of **Dwarf Rhododendrons** and related **woodland plants**.

The Nursery, sited in the old kitchen garden of **Holden Clough Hall**, still retains many of the original Victorian box hedges. It is very much an old-fashioned working nursery, not a garden centre, and there are display areas of **Alpine Raised Beds, Trough and Sink Gardens, Herbaceous Perennials** and **Shrubs**.

Whatever your requirements, staff will try and assist you in your choice of plant, and the Nursery is open all year, as stated in the advertisement, with the exception of Christmas to New Year, when the Nursery is closed.

Euphorbia Griffithii Fireglow at Holden Clough Nursery (HC)

Stydd Nursery

Hidden away off the beaten track on the edge of the historical and picturesque village of Ribchester is **Stydd Nursery**, a specialist plant nursery owned and run by **Len and Catherine Walker**, who established the business together at the end of the 1970s and now enjoy a national reputation for their plants.

Stydd Nursery is probably best known for its collection of **over 200 varieties of old-fashioned roses**, whose diversity of colour, shape, size and scent will astonish those gardeners accustomed only to the modern varieties seen so regularly in parks and garden centres. It is not just roses at Stydd Nursery, however. A wide range of **hardy herbaceous perennials** is also grown, as are **ornamental foliage plants** and a fascinating collection suitable for the house, greenhouse or conservatory. Included are many **scented-leaf pelargoniums** and **hardy geraniums**.

Visitors are able to wander at their leisure through an area of **display garden**, enjoying the plants and seeing them as they would develop in their own gardens. The roses are grown as a field crop. Bare root plants are available between November and March, but there are also a great many varieties grown in containers available for sale all year. Mr and Mrs Walker are pleased to assist with **advice on all aspects of gardening**, whether it be choosing plants for specific purposes, designing gardens or helping with pruning and other cultural problems.

Beautiful reflections in the nearby River Ribble at Ribchester

Making your visit complete...

Some Essential Services for the Visitor

Dales View
Caravan Park & Riding Centre

Props: Susan & Peter Tomlinson **Equestrian:** Elizabeth Tomlinson, B.H.S.I.I.

Situated right on the Lancashire-Yorkshire border & set amidst acres of breath taking scenery, Dales View Caravan Park & Riding Centre could not be better placed to enjoy that mixture of wild, rolling countryside, historic town & village life together with the convenience of modern shopping centres.

The Caravan Park Itself Is Very Well Equipped & Offers:
Toilet block with showers, basin & electrical points, telephone kiosk, launderette & washing up room, ample water points & Elsan facility, small games room & all mains service to statics.
Pony Trekking & Riding Tuition for all ages is available on site together with a variety of Equestrian Holidays.

For details contact: Dales View Caravan Park, Higher Lane, Salterforth, Nr Colne, Lancs. BB8 5SH. Telephone: 0282 816863

BROOKSIDE NURSERIES

For all your garden needs visit the highest nursery in the area - 1,000ft above sea level.

IF IT GROWS HERE - IT WILL GROW ANYWHERE

FOR A SUPERB SELECTION OF TREES, SHRUBS, ROSES, CONIFERS, HEATHERS, FRUIT TREES, ALPINES ETC

HOUSE PLANTS, FRESH & DRIED FLOWERS, GARDEN SUNDRIES.

HASLINGDEN OLD ROAD,
(A677 HASLINGDEN TO BLACKBURN)
NR. RISING BRIDGE ACCRINGTON TEL: (0706) 216491

HOLDEN CLOUGH NURSERY
(PETER J. FOLEY)

When visiting the Forest of Bowland, make sure and find time to spend an hour or more browsing through our well-stocked Frames and Display-Beds of ALPINES- HERBACEOUS PERENNIALS- FERNS-GRASSES-HEATHERS- DWARF SHRUBS-CLIMBERS AND DWARF CONIFERS.

This old established Nursery, always offers a very wide range of interesting and unusual varieties.
Our comprehensive catalogue is a good reference guide.

OPEN - Mon-Thurs 1.00-5.00pm
Sat & Bank Holiday Monday 9-5pm
(Last entry each day 4.30pm)

Dept. L. Holden, Nr. Bolton-by-Bowland, Clitheroe, Lancashire BB7 4PF. Tel: 0200 447615

STYDD NURSERY

Stonygate Lane, Ribchester,
Nr. Preston PR3 3YN
Tel: (0254) 878797

Open: Tues-Fri 1.30pm-5.00pm,
Sat 9.00am-5.00pm,
Sun (1st Apr-24th Dec) 2.00pm-5.00pm

Enjoy an afternoon in picturesque surroundings at our specialist plant nursery.

Features: • Display Garden - extensive collection of old fashioned roses & hardy perennials • Greenhouse - indoor/conservatory plants • Plant Sales Area • Advice • Information • Probably largest collection of old-fashioned roses in NW England.

A GUIDEBOOK TO MAKE YOUR VISIT TO THE RED ROSE COUNTY EVEN MORE ENJOYABLE

LANCASHIRE
The Red Rose County

Widely available throughout the North, or by mail order from:
MPS Ltd., 1 Market Place, Middleton-in-Teesdale,
Co. Durham, DL12 0QG. Tel: (0833) 40638

EXPLORE THE INDUSTRIAL HERITAGE AND RURAL DELIGHTS OF ENGLAND'S CENTRAL UPLANDS WITH THE HELP OF DISCOVERY GUIDES

THE SOUTH PENNINES

Widely available throughout the North, or by mail order from:
MPS Ltd., 1 Market Place, Middleton-in-Teesdale,
Co. Durham, DL12 0QG. Tel: (0833) 40638